Eat like a Viking!

A guide to Anglo Saxon & Viking age food & drink

By Craig Brooks

For my wife, Emma.

Always supportive and tolerant of my experimental food

For my daughter Ocean, my assistant veg chopper and fire lighter

Table of contents

'If some mouse or weasel fall into a large vessel of liquid, and is discovered there dead, sprinkle on some holy water and consume it as normal'

[Confessional of pseudo- Egbert]

Introduction

This guide was written as a small project for myself, to aid with my learning about early medieval food. I'm still fairly new to the subject, so hopefully there aren't too many errors and the book is of some use to people as a quick reference guide of available food types and gives some ideas for recipes to use while reenacting at events.

I found that the food would have been far from boring, with many farmed goods, as well as foraged and imported food stuffs. Daily food would have mainly consisted of savoury porridges and stews, flavoured with small quantities of meat.

Food would have been more seasonal than what we are used to now, with many produce only being available at certain times of year, unless it had been preserved by salting, pickling or drying.

Whilst we know a lot about the produce available, due to archeological finds, various writings and leechdoms, we don't know much about how they were eaten, with no recipe books being written until much later. We can summarise certain things from later cookbooks. For instance The Anglo Saxons were big fans of flowers in food. We know this because recipes from early Medieval France (before 1066) don't contain flowers, but the recipes that were written thereafter do.

Some of the recipes in this book, like the bread, can be made in advance of a show, with the benefit of using a modern kitchen, however I have tried to include the option to cook authentically where possible.

What follows is open to discussion, as these recipes are my take on what may or may not have been eaten by the Saxons and Vikings in the UK. It's been an interesting journey, experimenting with new ingredients, and new cooking methods, some of which have made it into our daily cooking routines, which I hope will give you some inspiration too.

With many thanks to David, Sue, Luke & Sarah of Moorforge, My wife Emma, Caroline Nicolay of Pario Gallico, and anyone else who helped with input, reading and ideas.

Cured salmon

Ingredients:

100g sea salt

80g honey

30g dill (finely chopped)

12 juniper berries (crushed)

A splash of mead

2 salmon fillets

Method:

Mix the Salt, honey, dill & berries well.

Place some cling film into a dish and lay 1 salmon fillet, skin side down and cover with the salt mix.

Place the second fillet, skin side up, on top and wrap tightly in the cling film.

Place something heavy on top and leave in the fridge for 2 - 4 days, depending on how salty you want the fish to be. Turn every 12 hours.

Drain any surplus liquid before serving

Oat wrapped cod

Ingredients:
Butter
2 cod fillets
1 egg
Salt and pepper
Rolled oats

Method:
Heat a little butter in a frying pan or on a griddle.

Whisk the egg and use it to coat the cod fillets. Season with salt & pepper.

Sprinkle some oats onto a plate and push the cod fillets firmly into them, turn the fillets over and coat the other side.

Fry for about 5 minutes. Carefully turn the fish and cook for a further 5 minutes, until cooked through

.

Pinnekjøt

Ingredients:
250g salt
Goat, lamb or pork ribs
Water
Birch sticks (bark removed)

Method:
To preserve;
Place the ribs in a large container and work the salt into the meat, making sure every part is covered.

Leave to rest somewhere cold or in the fridge for 24 hours per Kg. Turning every 12 hours.

Brush the excess salt off and hang in a cool & dry location. Dry for 4-6 weeks.

To cook;
Separate the ribs lengthwise and place to soak in cold water overnight.

In a large pan or cauldron build a grid with the birch sticks by criss-crossing the sticks in the bottom.

Add water to the pan, to just about cover the sticks. Place the ribs on top of the grid and pop a lid on the pan. Leave the meat to steam for 2-3 hours on a low heat. Be sure to add water occasionally to make sure it does not go dry. When the meat falls off the bone, it is done.

If you choose you can put the meat on a grill for about 15-20 minutes to crisp prior to serving.

Trout on a plank

Ingredients:
Water
A 2-3 cm thick plank of oak (big enough for a trout)
1 whole Trout
1 tsp fresh parsley (roughly chopped)
2 bay leaves

Method:
Soak the plank for 3 to 4 hours, or ideally overnight in water. You could substitute the water for beer or wine.

Prepare the fish by gutting, and removing the head, tail, and spine. Leave the 2 fillets attached to each other, making a 'butterfly'.

Clean the fish, place the bay leaves and parsley on the flesh of the trout and close the fillets, skin side out.

Place the trout onto the oak plank, and place the plank over hot coals.

Leave to slowly cook for about an hour until cooked through, flipping the fish half way through. The bottom of the wood will scorch and burn, cooking the fish through gentle steaming and lightly smoking.

Dried apple pieces

Ingredients:
Apples
String or canes

Method:
Core the apples and cut them into thin slices.

Thread them onto string or a cane, allowing a small gap between each piece. Hang them somewhere warm, near a fire is ideal.

Dry for a few days, or up to a week.

These can be eaten as a snack, or if you cut into small pieces they can be used to make a tea

Mint sauce

Ingredients:

A large bunch of mint

Pinch of salt

2 tablespoons of boiled water

1 tablespoon of honey

2 tablespoons of cider vinegar

Method:

Finely chop the mint. Add the salt, water, honey and vinegar. Mix well and leave to steep for 10 minutes before serving.

Salt dough lamb

Ingredients:
600g Flour
300g salt
Water
1/2 a Leg of lamb
Rosemary

Method:
Mix together the flour and salt and slowly add water, bringing it together to form a stiff dough.

Roll out the dough thin enough that it will encase the leg of lamb.

Make slits in the lamb with a sharp knife and stuff a little rosemary into the flesh.

Wrap the leg in the salt dough and cook for 2 hours (rare) up to 3 hours (well done) over hot coals, turning occasionally. Depending on conditions, this may need extra cooking time.

Remove the now burnt and blackened salt dough before serving.

Pork & Barley stew with dumplings

Ingredients:

For the stew;

A knob of Butter

300g pork (diced)

200ml cider

4 large handfuls of barley

2 turnips (peeled and and cut into chunks)

1 stick of celery (quartered and sliced)

1 leek (quartered and sliced)

A handful of kale

2 tsp black mustard seeds

1 sprig of rosemary (finely chopped)

A small bunch of thyme (finely chopped)

Salt & pepper (to taste)

For the dumplings (known as apples to the Saxons);

50g suet

100g flour

100ml cold water

Method:

Melt the butter in a large cooking pot. Add the pork and cook until nicely browning

Add the rest of the ingredients and add enough water to just cover everything.

Bring to the boil and simmer uncovered. Don't let the stew run dry, add a drop more water, if necessary.

While that's cooking. Mix together the suet and flour and season with salt & pepper. Slowly add the water, while mixing with your hands, until it all comes together.

Divide the dough into 4 and press firmly into balls. When the stew has been on for about 90 minutes, carefully drop the dumplings into the stew and simmer for a further 20 minutes.

Hall-stones

Ingredients:
100g butter
50g honey
1 egg
200g bread flour

Method:
Blend together the butter, honey and egg.

Mix in the flour to form a stiff dough.

Tip out onto a lightly floured work surface, and need together for several minutes.

Roll out the dough to about 1 cm thick, and cut into squares. Optionally, prick the tops with a knife.

Cook in the centre of a preheated oven at 180 degrees for about 10 - 15 minutes, until golden in colour.

Fish stew

Ingredients:
Butter
1 onion (finely chopped)
500ml hot fish stock
A few wild garlic leaves (finely chopped)
Parsley (finely chopped)
2 tsp fennel seeds
2 white or purple carrots (quartered and sliced)
375g mixed fish
165g raw prawns

Method:
Heat a little butter in a large pan or cauldron. Add the onion and fry for a few minutes, to soften.

Add the fish stock, herbs & carrot, bring to a boil, and simmer for about 20 minutes.

Add the mixed fish and cook for a further 10 minutes.

Finally add the prawns and cook for another 5 minutes, or until the prawns are pink and cooked through.

Serve immediately.

Pickled herrings

Ingredients:

1 herring (filleted and cut into bite size pieces)
1 Tablespoon salt
2 1/2 Cups water
1 cup cider vinegar
1 tablespoon of honey
2 tsp juniper berries
2 bay leaves
1 tsp mustard seeds
1 tsp black pepper

Method:

Heat the salt with 2 cups of water until dissolved. Leave to cool.

Add the herrings and leave to soak overnight.

Heat the rest of the ingredients together in a pan, bringing to a boil and simmering for 5 minutes. Leave to cool fully.

Once the Herring has finished soaking in the brine, drain and transfer to a suitable container.

Pour the vinegar over the top and leave for at least a week before eating.

Mussels

Ingredients:

Mussels
1/2 a pint of mead
250ml Cream
4 Spring onions (finely chopped)

Method:

Discard any open mussels that don't close when you tap them.

Mix together the mead and the cream. Stir in the onions.

Bring this to a boil and add the Mussels. Cover and leave to cook for 2 minutes.

Remove the cover and shake or stir. When all the mussels have opened they are ready.

Venison stew

Ingredients:

Butter

1 Onion (finely chopped)

500g diced Venison

500ml beef or venison stock

1 Leek (sliced)

2 parsnips

2 sticks of Celery (sliced)

1 Turnip (diced)

Handful of roughly chopped Kale

Splash of Elderberry wine or red wine

2 Bay leaves

2 tsp finely chopped fresh thyme

1 sprig of Rosemary

1 stick of Cinnamon

Method:

Heat a little butter in a large pan or cauldron. Add the onion and fry for a few minutes, to soften.

Add the venison, stock, veg, wine & herbs, bring to a boil, and simmer for about 2 hours., topping up with more water if necessary.

Remove the bay, rosemary and cinnamon and serve immediately.

Nettle & wild garlic soup

Ingredients:

A knob of Butter

1 onion (finely chopped)

2 sticks of celery (finely chopped)

2 carrots (finely chopped)

2 large handfuls of young nettle tops (finely chopped)

1 large handful of wild garlic leaves (finely chopped)

1L stock

3 tablespoons of full fat milk or cream

Salt & pepper (to taste)

Method:

Heat the butter in a pan. Add the onion and cook for several minutes, until softening.

Add the celery, carrots, nettles, wild garlic and stock.

Bring to a boil and simmer for about 20 minutes.

Stir in the milk and serve with crusty sourdough bread.

Chicken & Ginger soup

Ingredients:

A knob of Butter

1 onion (roughly chopped)

600g Chicken breast (cut into chunks)

1L chicken stock

2 carrots (quartered and sliced)

2 sticks of celery (roughly chopped)

A small bunch of wild garlic leaves (Finely chopped)

1 thumb sized piece of ginger (Finely chopped)

Method:

Melt the butter in a large pan or cauldron. Add the onion and fry for a few minutes to soften.

Add the chicken and fry for a few minutes.

Pour over the chicken stock and add the carrots, celery, garlic and ginger. Bring to a boil and simmer for about 20 minutes.

Serve with fresh sourdough bread

Stuffed spit roasted heart

Ingredients:

2 lambs hearts

For the stuffing;

Butter

200g lardons

Large handful of hazelnuts (finely chopped)

Large handful of spinach

1 mushroom (finely chopped)

Splash of white wine (parsnip if you have it)

Method:

Melt some butter in a pan. Add the lardons and fry for several minutes, until browning.

Add the rest of the stuffing ingredients and fry, Stirring occasionally, until the liquid has cooked off and the spinach is wilted.

Leave to one side to cool.

Trim the hearts of any excess fat and slice them in half, but not all the way through, opening them up like a butterfly.

Spoon some of the stuffing mix onto the open hearts, close them up and tie together with a few pieces of string.

Push the hearts onto a skewer and cook for around 30 - 40 minutes over a hot fire, depending on how rare you like it.

Leave to rest for 5 minutes, before slicing and serving with any leftover stuffing mix.

Walnut & apple salad

Ingredients:

1 tablespoon of Cider vinegar

1 tablespoon of Olive oil

2 apples (Finely chopped)

2 handfuls of walnuts (roughly chopped)

2 large spoonfuls of soft cheese

Handful of wild garlic leaves

2 large handfuls of Spinach

2 large handfuls of Rocket

Method:

Mix together the vinegar and oil.

Mix the remainder of the ingredients and drizzle with the vinegar/oil mix

Buttered turnips

Ingredients:
3 turnips
large knob of butter
splash of milk

Method:
Peel and cut the turnips into chunks

Add to a cooking pot or cauldron, cover with water and boil for 10 -15 minutes until soft.

Drain, add the butter and milk and mash using either the back of a spoon or the Tvare whisk found later in this book (page 79)

Beef Jerky

Ingredients:
220g beef
4 tablespoon cider vinegar
1 tablespoon honey
2 tsp juniper berries
1/2 tsp cinnamon
1 tsp salt
1 tsp pepper

Method:
Freeze the beef for about 45 minutes, this will make slicing it easier.

Slice the beef as thinly as possible and place in a suitable container for marinading.

Mix together the rest of the ingredients and pour over the beef.

Marinade for a couple of hours.

Heat your oven to 80 degrees Celsius.

Remove the beef from the marinade and place in a single layer in the oven.

Cook for 2-2.5 hours, until dry.

Pig tail soup

Ingredients:

3 pig tails (cut into 1-1.5" chunks)

1.5L chicken stock

1 onion (finely chopped)

3 carrots (quartered and diced)

3 handfuls of split peas

3 celery (finely chopped)

Handful of wild garlic (roughly chopped)

2 bay leaves

Butter

Method:

Stick the pig tails in a pan or cauldron. Add the stock.

Bring to a boil & simmer for 40 minutes. Add the rest of the ingredients and cook for a further
20 minutes.

Remove from the heat and remove the tails from the soup.

Heat some butter in a pan and fry the tails for 10-20 minutes, until crispy. Return the tails to the soup and serve

Soft fresh cheese

Ingredients:
1L Full fat milk (I like to use goat)
250ml buttermilk/1-2 tablespoons of vinegar or rennet
Salt

Method:
Heat the milk until almost boiling.

Take off the heat, add the buttermilk, vinegar or rennet and stir thoroughly.

Leave for about 15 minutes. The milk will curdle and the whey and curds will separate.

Pour the mixture through a sieve or colander, lined with a double layer of cheesecloth.

Rinse with cold water and sprinkle a little salt over the cheese.

Leave to drain for about 2 hours.

This will keep, if chilled, for up to a week, but the flavour will mature.

Garlic mushrooms

Ingredients:

Butter

A few mushrooms (ideally locally foraged)

A small bunch of wild garlic leaves or flowers, or modern cloves work too (finely chopped)

1/2 tsp rosemary (finely chopped)

1/2 tsp thyme (finely chopped)

Salt & pepper (to taste)

Method:

Melt a little butter in a pan.

Roughly chop the mushrooms and add them to the pan.

Fry for a couple of minutes, before adding the rest of the ingredients.

Fry once more for a couple of minutes before serving. I like mine with eggs.

Sausages

Ingredients:
Recipe 1;
240g venison
60g pork fat
1 tsp wild garlic
½ an onion
½ tsp of salt
¼ tsp freshly ground pepper
Sausage casings (soaked in cold water and rinsed)

Recipe 2;
240g Pork
60g pork fat
1 tsp summer savory
½ tsp salt
¼ tsp freshly ground pepper
Sausage casings (soaked in cold water and rinsed)

Method:

Chop the ingredients up as finely as possible, then knead and mash the ingredients together for a few minutes. If you have a sausage maker you could grind the meat through this to save a lot of time.

Push one end of your pre soaked sausage casing over a sausage horn (see page 85) and tie the loose end.

Stuff the ingredients through the horn into the casing. This is a slow process, don't rush or overfill the casing, or it might split.

Twist the sausage at even intervals to mark out individual sausages. If there is any trapped air in the sausages prick the skin with a small needle or pin.

To cook these, boil them in water (or try stock or beer) for 10-15 minutes, until cooked through. Alternatively, though less authentic for the time, they can be grilled or fried.

Sage & cheese omelette

Ingredients:
2 eggs
A knob of butter
A small bunch of fresh sage (roughly chopped)
A handful of grated cheese
Salt & Pepper

Method:
Whisk the eggs until they're combined.

Melt the butter in a frying pan and add the eggs, making sure to spread them around the pan.

Cook the eggs until they start to set. Add the sage and cheese, evenly, to the top of the omelette and season with salt & pepper.

Fold gently in half and slide onto a plate to serve.

Elderflower pottage

Ingredients:
1 cup almonds (finely chopped or crushed)
1 cups boiled water
1 cups of oats
1 Elderflower head, storks removed (or other edible flowers)
A few slices of apple (roughly chopped)
1 tablespoon honey
1 knob butter
2 egg yolks

Method:
Soak the almonds in the water for about 15 minutes.

Add the rest of the ingredients and bring to a boil. Simmer until it reaches the desired consistency. Much like porridge this varies from person to person.

Rosemary flower omelette

Ingredients:
½ a small onion (finely chopped)
2 eggs
Butter
A handful of fresh rosemary flowers
A small bunch of fresh garlic leaves (roughly chopped)
Salt & Pepper

Method:
Melt some butter in a frying pan and add the onion. Fry for 5-10 minutes until caramelising.

Remove from the pan and leave to one side.

Whisk the eggs until they're combined.

Melt some butter in a frying pan and add the eggs, making sure to spread them around the pan.

Cook the eggs until they start to set. Add the onions, rosemary flowers and garlic, evenly, to the top of the omelette

Fold gently in half and slide onto a plate to serve.

Honey & oat cakes

Ingredients:
200g unsalted butter
200g honey
500g oats
1/4 cup of liquid (braggot, ale, mead, milk etc) *(½ cup)*
1 apple (finely chopped) *(maybe 2) (or w/ berries)*
1 tsp ground cinnamon

Method:
Melt the butter in a pan. Stir in the honey, followed by the rest of the ingredients.

Mix together well and leave to cool. Once cool, split the mixture into even sized amounts. Roll into balls and squash each ball as flat as possible.

Cook for a few minutes on each side on a hot griddle or frying pan. Watch them carefully, or they will burn.

Alternatively heat your oven to 170 degrees and cook in the centre of the oven for approx 10 - 15 minutes, until firm and golden in colour.

Leave to cool fully before eating, as they will firm up when cool.

Pickled veg

Ingredients:
Recipe 1;
2 parsnips (sliced)
1 tsp salt
300ml Cider vinegar
1 tablespoon honey
1 tsp mustard seeds
1 tsp black peppercorns

Recipe 2;
2 handfuls of kale
1 tsp salt
300ml Cider vinegar
1 tablespoon honey
1 tsp caraway seeds
1 tsp black peppercorns

Method:

Sprinkle the salt over the vegetables and mix well. Pack into warm, sterile jars or another suitable container.

Bring the vinegar to a boil in a pan with the honey and simmer for a few minutes.

Pour into the jars, completely covering the vegetables. Add the seeds and peppercorns.

Seal the jar or container immediately and leave to pickle for at least 2 weeks before using. These make a great addition to soups and stews.

Hawthorn sauce

Ingredients:
500g Hawthorn berries
350g cider apple vinegar
350ml water
200g honey
½ tsp salt
½ a tsp pepper

Method:
Heat the berries with the vinegar and water. Bring to a boil and simmer for 30 minutes.

Strain through a sieve, pushing the berries through with a spoon, discarding the seeds and skin.

Return to the heat with the rest of the ingredients and simmer until the thickness of ketchup.

Strain through a sieve into clean, sterile bottles or jars. This should keep for around a year.

This sauce makes a great accompaniment to dark meats, like venison or gamey birds like Pigeon.

Hazelnut patties

Ingredients:
100g butter
100g honey
2 eggs
200g hazelnuts (finely chopped or crushed)
200g flour

Method:
Cream together the butter, honey and eggs.

Stir in the hazelnuts and flour. Kneed together to form a slightly sticky dough.

Split the mixture into even sized amounts. Roll into balls and squash each ball as flat as possible.

Cook for a few minutes on each side on a hot griddle or frying pan. Watch them carefully, or they will burn.

Alternatively heat your oven to 170 degrees and cook in the centre of the oven for approx 10 to 15 minutes, until firm and golden in colour

Leave to cool fully before eating, as they will firm up when cool.

Egg custard tarts

Ingredients:

300g plain flour (sifted)

150g unsalted butter (cut into cubes)

Water

250ml whole milk

250ml Full fat cream

4 egg yolks

80g honey

Cinnamon

Method:
Add the butter to the flour and rub it between your fingers and into the flour. Keep rubbing until the mix resembles breadcrumbs.

Add a small drop of water and mix together. Keep adding a little water at a time, until the mixture comes together to form a stiff dough and leaves the bowl mostly clean.

On a lightly floured surface, roll the pastry out as thin as possible - 1 or 2 mm is best. Cut rounds for the bases using a pastry cutter and place into cupcake cases.

Blind bake (filling each pie with dry beans) for 10 minutes at 180 degrees, remove the beans and cook for a further 5 minutes at 160 degrees.

Remove from the oven.

Heat the milk and cream together until almost boiling.

Beat the egg yolks with the honey, then whisk in the hot milk.

Pour the custard into the baked pastry cases and sprinkle a little cinnamon on top.

Bake for around 20 minutes at 140 degrees until the custard has set.

.

Split pea pottage

Pottage would have been quite a common food for the Anglo Saxons and Vikings. Often left in the pot for days or even weeks, with new ingredients added as they went along. This is a great base pottage, but feel free to add your own ingredients as you go along.

Ingredients:
Butter
6 rashers of Bacon (roughly chopped)
1 leek (roughly chopped)
2 sticks of celery (roughly chopped)
1.5L chicken stock (any stock will work)
300g Dried split peas
Handful of wild garlic (finely 3chopped)
2 tsp fresh mint (roughly chopped)

Method:
Melt some butter in a large pan or cauldron.

Add the bacon and cook for a few minutes, until starting to brown. Add the leeks and celery and fry for a few minutes.

Pour in the stock and add the peas, garlic and mint.

Bring to a boil and simmer for about an hour, until reduced by a third and the peas are soft. If necessary top up with more water.

Butter

Ingredients:
Double cream (at room temperature)

Method:
Put the cream into a bowl.

Mix and stir vigorously with a whisk, or your hand for 5 - 10 minutes, the cream will thicken, then suddenly start to slosh around as the buttermilk separates from the butter.

Drain the buttermilk, and stir again for another minute to remove the last of the buttermilk, before draining one last time.

Rinse the butter with cold water. Optionally you can now season with salt or try adding herbs or garlic to the butter.

The buttermilk can be used for making cheese, cakes or biscuits.

Smoked mackerel butter

Ingredients:

Smoked mackerel fillets (skin and bones removed)

Unsalted butter (about half the same volume as fish)

A mix of salad leaves, such as garlic-mustard, wild garlic, rocket, watercress (finely chopped)

Method:

Flake the fish into a bowl

Add the fresh butter and work together into a paste, until smooth. Add more butter if too stiff.

Add the salad leaves and mix well.

Serve on warm fresh bread, flat breads or oat cakes

Pancakes

Ingredients:
100g plain flour (sifted)
2 eggs
300ml milk
Pinch of salt
Butter

Optional - Spring flowers (hawthorn, elderflower etc) or finely chopped blanched greens (nettles, rocket, spinach etc).

Method:
Whisk together all the ingredients until smooth. Stir in any extras, if using.

Melt some butter in a pan and add a ladle full of batter to the pan.

Cook for a minute or 2 on each side, until golden brown.

If you have a sweet tooth, serve with honey. Nettle and honey is lovely.

Crisp breads

Ingredients:
300g flour (plus a little extra for dusting the worktop)
10g Salt
10g Cumin **or** fennel seeds (roughly ground in a pestle & mortar)
water

Method:
Mix together the dry ingredients in a bowl. Slowly add water and mix to form a dough.

Flour your worktop with a little flour and roll the dough out thinly. Cut the dough into rounds and make a hole in the middle.

Place onto a baking tray that has been lined with greaseproof paper.

Cook in the centre of a preheated oven at 200 degrees for about 20 – 30 minutes until lightly browned and crisp. Remove from the oven and leave to cool.

Flatbread

Ingredients:
100g bread flour + a little extra
2g salt
60 ml water (give or take)
Optional - Small bunch of roughly chopped herbs or fruit/nuts, for example; nettles/rosemary/walnuts or a tsp of fennel/cumin seed etc

Method:
Put the flour and salt into a large bowl and mix together.

Add any extras (if using) and slowly add the water and mix together to form a workable dough. You can add more or less water depending on how your dough feels. I find it varies slightly every time.

Tip out onto your worktop, dust your hands with flour and knead for 5 minutes.

Roll the dough into a ball and dust with a little flour.

Flatten to around 0.5-1 cm thick.

Cook for 3 or 4 minutes on each side in a hot frying pan, without any oil.

Sourdough starter

This is a simple way of making bread using naturally occurring yeasts.

If you want to give your starter an extra kickstart and additional flavour, try adding a small amount of the lees from fermenting beer or mead.

You will need a large container, flour (any kind, but rye and wholemeal seem to ferment easiest) and warm water. I don't tend to measure what I add but you are looking for a thick batter, so around 50/50 works well. Give it a good whisk, cover loosely and set it aside.

After a couple of days you should see signs of fermentation, tiny bubbles and if you smell it, it should be taking on a sharp, fruity, vinegary smell. Add some more flour and water, whisk and set it aside again.

Remember that your starter is now a living thing, so, like you, it needs feeding and watering regularly, I do it every couple of days. You can remove some of your starter, as you wish, which makes a great opportunity to bake some bread with it!

Wait a week to 10 days for the starter to establish properly before trying to bake with it.

Saxon bread

Ingredients:
780g bread flour (plus a little extra for coating)
10g salt
26g honey
250g sourdough starter
Warm water

Method:
Put the flour and salt, into a large bowl and mix together.

Add the honey and starter and slowly add enough water to mix together to form a dough. It needs to be workable, so as not to stick to your hands too much, but too dry and it will fall apart. You can add more or less water depending on how your dough feels. I find it varies slightly every time.

Tip out onto a work surface and knead for around 5-10 minutes.

Roll your dough into a ball, and dust with a little flour. Put it into a bowl and cover loosely with a damp cloth, to stop it drying out. Leave to prove for at least several hours, but overnight is ideal.

Sourdough takes longer to develop than bread made with shop bought yeast, but benefits from the extra time, as it develops a better flavour. The loaf should increase in size.

Tip your dough back out onto your work surface and carefully deflate it by poking it with your fingers.

Shape your dough into a loaf, and dust with a little flour. Place onto a lightly flour dusted oven tray and prove for another hour.

Heat your oven to its highest temperature.

Cook for 10 minutes before dropping the temperature to 200 degrees if the crust is looking pale, 180 degrees if the crust is noticeably browning, and 170 if it seems to be browning quickly. Cook for a further 40 mins.

Remove from the oven, the loaf should sound hollow when you tap it on the bottom.

This can also be cooked in the dying embers of a fire, just divide the dough into small rolls first, rather than a loaf.

Leave to cool fully before cutting.

Nettle bread

Ingredients:

Large handful of finely chopped nettle tops

350g bread flour (plus extra for dusting)

1 Tsp salt

7g yeast

100 ml milk

50 ml water

Method:
Put the nettles, flour and salt into a large bowl and mix together. Add the yeast.

Mix together the water and milk.

Slowly add the milk solution to the bowl of dry ingredients and mix together to form a dough.

You can add more or less milk/water depending on how your dough feels. I find it varies slightly every time.

Tip out onto your worktop and knead for around 10 minutes.

Roll your dough into a ball, and dust with a little flour. Put it into a bowl and cover loosely with a damp cloth, to stop it drying out. Place somewhere warm.

Leave to prove for 1-2 hours, or until the dough has roughly doubled in size.

Tip your dough back out onto your work surface and carefully deflate it by poking it with your fingers. Divide the mix into 4 equal pieces. Roll each piece into a ball and coat with a little more flour.

Place onto a baking tray, that has been dusted with flour, and leave for another hour or to prove again.

Heat your oven to 200 degrees Celsius.

Cook for about 20 minutes.

Remove from the oven, the rolls should sound hollow when you tap them on the bottom.

These can also be cooked in the dying embers of a fire.

Leave to cool fully before serving with butter.

Black bread

Ingredients:

3 tsp dry blood (ask a butcher or check Amazon)

200ml warm water

500g bread flour (+ extra for coating)

10g salt

200g sourdough starter

50g honey

Method:

Mix the dried blood with the water and whisk to a smooth consistency.

Put the flour and salt into a large bowl and mix together. Add the starter and honey and slowly add the blood solution and mix together to form a dough. You can add more or less water depending on how your dough feels. I find it varies slightly every time.

Tip out onto your worktop and knead for around 10 minutes.

Roll your dough into a ball, and dust with a little flour. Put it into a bowl and cover loosely with a damp cloth, to stop it drying out. Place somewhere warm.

Leave to prove for 3-4 hours, until the dough has roughly doubled in size.

Tip your dough back out onto your work surface and carefully deflate it by poking it with your fingers. Divide the mix into 8 equal pieces. Roll each piece into a ball and coat with a little flour.

Place onto a baking tray, that has been dusted with flour, and leave for another hour or to prove again.

Heat your oven to 200 degrees Celsius and cook for about 20 minutes.

Remove from the oven, the rolls should sound hollow when you tap them on the bottom.

These can also be cooked in the dying embers of a fire.

Leave to cool fully before serving with butter.

Walnut & honey bread

Ingredients:
200g wholemeal bread flour
300 strong white bread flour
10g salt
100g walnuts (roughly chopped)
200g sourdough starter
50g honey
250ml warm water (give or take)

Method:
Put the flour, walnuts and salt into a large bowl and mix together.

Add the starter, and honey. Slowly add the water and mix together to form a dough.

It needs to be workable, so as not to stick to your hands too much, but too dry and it will fall apart. You can add more or less water depending on how your dough feels. I find it varies slightly every time.

Tip out onto your worktop and knead for around 5-10 minutes. I don't bother to flour or oil the worktop, I never really found it necessary.

There are various ways to knead your dough I like to stretch it out, then roll it back in and give it a 90 degree turn, before stretching it out again.

Cover with a damp cloth and leave to prove, somewhere warm, for a couple of hours, or until it has roughly doubled in size.

Tip the dough back onto your work surface and shape into a loaf, place on a baking tray.

Leave the loaf to prove for a further 30 minutes. Meanwhile, pre-heat the oven to 250 degrees C.

Slash the top of the loaf, and leave to prove for a further 10 minutes.

Pour some boiled water on the bottom of the oven.

Cook for 10 minutes before dropping the temperature to 200 degrees if the crust is looking pale, 180 degrees if the crust is noticeably browning, and 170 if it seems to be browning quickly. Cook for a further 40 mins.

Remove from the oven, the loaf should sound hollow when you tap it on the bottom, if not return it to the oven for a little longer.

This can also be cooked in the dying embers of a fire, just divide the dough into small rolls first, rather than a loaf.

Leave to cool fully before cutting.

Rye bread

Ingredients:

300g rye flour

100g white bread flour

100g sourdough starter

1 tsp salt

300ml warm water (give or take)

1 tablespoon caraway seeds

Method:
Put the flour and salt into a large bowl and mix together.

Add the starter and slowly add the water and mix together to form quite a sticky dough that is more like a cake mix than a bread dough. You can add more or less water depending on how your dough feels. I find it varies slightly every time.

Add the seeds and mix well. There is no point kneading this bread.

Place the dough in a lightly greased loaf tin. Cover loosely with a damp cloth and leave for a few hours, ideally overnight. It won't rise very much due to the low gluten content of the rye flour.

Heat your oven to its highest temperature.

Put your loaf in the centre of the oven for 10 minutes before dropping the temperature to 200 degrees Celsius if the crust is looking pale, 180 degrees Celsius if the crust is noticeably browning, and 170 degrees Celsius if it seems to be browning quickly. Cook for a further 40 mins.

Remove from the tin. The loaf should sound hollow when you tap it on the bottom.

Leave to cool fully before cutting.

Sourdough crumpets

Modern crumpets use Bicarb to add bubbles, so if not making authentically you could add a tsp to the mix.

Ingredients:
200g sourdough starter
20g bread flour
1 tsp honey
1 tsp salt
butter

Method:
Mix the starter, flour, honey and salt in a large jug or bowl. Cover with a wet cloth or tea towel and leave to prove for about an hour.

Put a couple of crumpet rings into a frying pan, and grease well with butter.

Heat the butter on a low heat and, once hot, add 1 tablespoon of batter to each ring. Cook for around 5 minutes, until the top is full of tiny air bubbles.

Carefully remove the hot ring, flip and fry for a further few minutes, until golden in colour and cooked through.

Re-oil the rings for each crumpet made, to avoid the crumpets sticking.

Raspberry/Blackberry leaf tea

Method:

Pick only the young, fresh looking new leaves.

Wash and then bruise the leaves with a rolling pin.

Store in an airtight container for 3-6 weeks to 'ferment'

Lay the leaves out in a single layer to dry somewhere warm until crunchy.

Crumble the leaves into small pieces and store somewhere dry.

To make a tea, add 1 teaspoon per cup of hot water. Strain before drinking.

Nettle leaf tea

Method:

Wear stout gloves and pick only the young, fresh looking new leaves. The top 3 or 4, in spring is ideal.

Wash and lay the leaves out in a single layer to dry somewhere warm until crunchy.

Crumble the leaves into small pieces and store somewhere dry.

To make a tea, add 1 teaspoon per cup of hot water. Strain before drinking.

Dandelion flower tea

Method:

Collect a few handfuls of dandelion flowers on a warm sunny day if possible.

Wash the flowers and remove the green parts, as these will make the tea bitter.

Put 2 teaspoons of flower petals per cup of tea. Pour boiling water over the top, and let the tea steep for a few minutes. Strain before drinking.

Serve with honey to taste.

Getting started with home-brew

The first rule of making any kind of brew, is to make sure you sterilise everything. Buckets, bottles, siphons – everything that comes into contact with your brew. You can buy sterilising powder in home-brew shops, Wilko's or online. Follow the directions on the packet and clean everything thoroughly.
Once clean, rinse the equipment well.

The next thing is to make sure you have a hydrometer. These are cheap to buy and will help you to know when your brew is finished fermenting. It will also enable you to estimate the alcohol content of your finished brew.

- Take a reading before you add your yeast. This is known as the Original gravity or OG
- Take another at the end. This is known as the Final gravity or FG
- Using a simple formula, (OG – FG) x 0.13 = %, you can then figure out the alcohol content of your finished brew
- For example if your original gravity is 1080 and your final gravity is 1000, then using the formula (1080 – 1000) x 0.13 = 10.4% alcohol content

The original gravity of most wines and meads should start at around 1050 – 1100

The original gravity for beer should start at around 1040

The higher the number, the higher the potential alcohol content of your brew, however this is also limited by the type of yeast used.

Your brew will either finish fermenting when the yeast runs out of food (sugar) or when the alcohol content is too high for the yeast to live in.

When your brew stops bubbling, or slows to less than 1 bubble a minute, use the hydrometer to see if your brew is finished fermenting. Move your brew somewhere warm and check the gravity over a period of 3 days and if the reading doesn't change, fermentation has stopped.

At this stage there are a few optional things you can add to your brew. The first 2 things are fermentation stopper, and campden tablets. These are generally added at the same time to wine, mead and cider, and help to stabilise the alcohol by killing off any yeast that might still be hanging around. They also help to prevent any bacterial growth during the ageing process. Add these as per the packet instructions, usually you'll need to stir your brew daily for 3 days after adding, which will also help to remove any trapped co2.

The next thing is bentonite. This is a naturally occurring clay that draws particles from the alcohol and settles it to the bottom of your container. This clears the alcohol, so you can siphon your liquid into a new container or bottle to prevent a hazy wine.

Meadowsweet mead

Ingredients:
1.8Kg honey
30g meadowsweet
4.5 l water
1 teaspoon of wine yeast

Method:
Put half the honey into a clean, sterile bucket with the meadowsweet.

Pour in 4.5 litres of boiled water and stir until the honey is dissolved.

When the liquid has cooled to room temperature, add the yeast. Leave to ferment for 2 days.

Strain the liquid through a clean muslin into a demijohn, fit with an airlock and leave to ferment for a further 5 days.

Syphon the mead into a clean demijohn, leaving behind any sediment.
Add the rest of the honey and mix well.

When fermentation ends (bubbles passing through the airlock at less than one a minute) siphon the mead into bottles and cork.

Age for a minimum of 3 months before drinking.

Braggot

Ingredients:

30g hops

1362g honey

500g amber malt extract

12 pints water

Method:

Put the hops into a large pan and cover with 6 pints of water, boil for 30 minutes.

Meanwhile put your honey and malt extract into a large, sterilised bucket or fermentation bin. Strain the hop water through a muslin cloth into the fermentation bin.

Stir well to dissolve all the honey and malt extract. Pour in 6 pints of cold water and stir.

Check your gravity, it should be around 1060. If not you can adjust up or down by adding more honey or water, as necessary. This should give you a braggot around 7.8%.

Add your yeast and leave to ferment for 2 to 3 weeks.

Don't forget to check your final gravity, if you haven't already and want to know the percentage of alcohol in your brew.

Sterilise your bottles.

Add a ½ teaspoon of honey to each bottle and siphon the beer into the bottles. Cap the bottles (or use swing tops) and place somewhere warm for 2 days before moving to somewhere cool.

The braggot should be ready to drink in 2 weeks, 3 is better.

Yarrow Ale

This is a modern recipe with a nod to authentic beer brewing. For more authentic brewing, leave out the sugar, as this would not have been available. You could add honey instead, but this will be more like the previous recipe for braggot.

Without sugar the beer will be a lot weaker, maybe 1 or 2 percent, and so will not keep for long. This would have been made frequently and drunk within a few days at most.

Ingredients:
10g Bog myrtle
10g Yarrow
500g Amber malt extract
475g sugar
12 pints of water
1 teaspoon wine yeast

Method:
Put the bog myrtle and yarrow into a large pan and cover with 6 pints of water, boil for 30 minutes.

Meanwhile put your sugar and malt extract into a large, sterilised, bucket or fermentation bin. Strain the hop water through a muslin cloth into the fermentation bin.

Stir well to dissolve all the sugar and malt extract. Pour in 6 pints of cold water and stir.

Check your gravity, it should be around 1040. If not you can adjust up or down by adding more sugar or water, as necessary. This should give you an ale of around 5.2%.

Add your yeast and leave to ferment for 2 to 3 weeks.

Don't forget to check your final gravity, if you haven't already and want to know the percentage of alcohol in your brew.

Sterilise your bottles.

Add ½ a level teaspoon of sugar to each bottle and siphon the beer into the bottles. Cap the bottles (or use swing tops) and place somewhere warm for 2 days before moving to somewhere cool.

The beer should be ready to drink in 2 weeks, 3 is better.

Elderberry mead

Ingredients:

1500g elderberries

4.5l water (boiled)

1.5 kg honey

1 tsp pectic enzyme

1 tsp of red wine yeast

1 tsp yeast nutrient

Method:
Put all the berries into a large bucket and crush with a rolling pin. Add the honey, and pectic enzyme and cover with 4.5l boiled water. Stir well.

Once cool, make a note of your gravity.

Add your yeast and nutrient and cover loosely for 1 week before straining into a demijohn with an airlock.

When fermentation ends (bubbles passing through the airlock at less than one a minute) check your final gravity.

Finally, syphon the wine into bottles and cork.

Age for a minimum of 6 months before drinking, but a year is better.

.

Whisk: version 1

Traditional Scandinavian tvare whisks date back to at least the 9th century. The old Norse word for them was *þvara.*

The word *tvare*, means 'mixing' though they would have been used for mashing, as well as stirring porridge and stew.

As these were custom made the size of the handle varied for its user, as well as its purpose.

The handle can be anything up to half a metre long for large pots of porridge.

1. The first step is to find a suitable tree, the top part of a 5 foot tree will probably make no more than two whisks, any lower down the handle and branches will be too thick to work with.
2. Cut the trunk to the desired length for your handle. Cut below the second large spread of branches. Remove the top branches and any others along the stem.
3. Cut the remaining branches to around 5/6cm long.
4. Remove as much bark as possible from the handle and branches. Don't worry too much as this will be easier after the next step.
5. Bring a large pan of water to a boil and boil the wood for 10-15 minutes. This will soften the remaining bark, making it easier to remove.
6. The final step is to sand everything smooth and treat with a food safe oil. Traditionally this would be Linseed.

I have been advised to leave the whisk to dry for a considerable time before using, as it does tend to impart a certain floor cleaner flavour to your food.

Whisk: version 2

Some old recipes call for a particular type of tree branch to be used, to add a particular flavour to a cake. Whatever type you choose, be sure to remove all traces of bark, or you'll end up with bits in your food!

To make simply bind together a bundle of food safe sticks at one end. Shorter sticks will be harder to whisk with, but it's worth experimenting with different lengths to find what suits you.

Elderberry fire bellows

The word "Elder" is derived from the Anglo-saxon words 'aeld' (fire) and 'Eldrun' (furnace). The hollow stems were used to blow air into the hearth

Cut an approximately 2cm thick branch of elderberry wood to around 70 cm long, it can be slightly longer, but much shorter will hinder its use, blowing smoke into your face, as I found with my first attempt!

Remove the outer bark, hollow out the soft middle using a long piece of stiff wire, or a long drill bit

Char cloth

Used to light fires with just a spark. It works incredibly well and burns very hot. It's also easy to make and can be used for authentic fire lighting for reenactment purposes. All you need is some 100% cotton or linen cloth - an old dust sheet works well, though I have heard that denim or old flannels are good, as well as cheesecloth or muslin.

1. Cut the cloth into rough squares, 2" works well.
2. Put the squares into a tin. Any can work, providing it has a tight seal and doesn't have any rubber or plastic seals. Try an old sweet or mint tin.
3. Don't pack the tin too tightly, I learned this my first time, as things don't burn evenly and I ended up having to start again.
4. Punch a hole in the tin lid using a 6" nail. This allows gasses to escape, without too much oxygen getting in and turning the cloth to ashes.
5. Stick the tin onto a heat source (outdoors due to the smoke produced). I use a small gas camping stove.
6. After a few minutes of heating, smoke will stream from the hole in the lid, which may also ignite at times, but don't worry, this is normal.
7. Continue to burn until the smoke is no longer coming from the hole - anywhere from 5-15 minutes.
8. Remove from the heat, but do not remove the lid until the contents are completely cool. I learned this the hard way. By removing the lid and allowing oxygen into the tin, the cloth will combust.
9. Once the tin is cool and you have removed the cloth, store in an airtight container and keep dry until needed.
10. To ignite all you need is a spark from a flint and steel and some tinder. Straw, dried nettles or Gorse work well.

.

Sausage stuffer

Use the cut end of a piece of horn to aid the stuffing of sausage cases. An old drinking horn works well. It needs to be small enough to fit a casing on to, but with an opening large enough to stuff meat through. Mine measures approximately 2" long by 1" at its narrowest. The opening at the small end is about 1/2 inch, but find what works for you.

When you cut the horn, you may need to use a drill to open up the hole a little more.

Available food types

This book started with this list. I still use it now as a quick reference guide and hopefully it will be of some use to you as well. Whilst this is not a definitive list, it covers a wide range of food that we know was available, due to writings from the time and archeological finds.

Fruits, Nuts & seeds

An important food type, whether farmed, imported or foraged. The word harvest comes from the Old English word 'haerfest' meaning Autumn.

Some nuts would have been solely used as feed for livestock, or to make flour, meal and oils, particularly in times of famine. Fruits would have been fermented, as well as eaten fresh.

Acorns - Foraged. Contain high levels of tannin and can be toxic unless treated first by soaking several times to remove tannin and processing into flour/meal. Probably eaten mainly during famine or used to feed livestock. Charred acorns found in a Saxon hut in Stevenage.

Almonds - Mentioned in Leechdoms as 'suitable for sensitive stomachs' hinting at edibility though use may not be widespread due to lack of other evidence. May be reserved for the wealthy?

Apples - Foraged and farmed. Eaten and preserved, fermented to make cider and vinegar. Widespread archeological evidence at many sites including 4 small crab apples at Ford (Wilts), and pips at York, Hedeby, Kaupang and Oseberg.

Beech-mast - Foraged. Can be eaten raw or toasted. Due to the high fat content they have been processed into oil for cooking and lighting or ground to make coffee. Also used as animal feed. Found in a grave at Hitchen.

Bilberries - Sometimes known as whortleberry, wild blueberry or whinberry. Foragable. Evidence at York and Lofoten and rare mention in Leechdoms.

Blackberries - Known as bramble apples to the Saxons. Found at York, Hedeby and Kaupang

Cherries - Finds at London, Hamwih and York. Wild cherries found at Hedeby.

Dewberries - Related to the blackberry, but similar in flavour to Raspberries. Found at York

Elderberries - To the Saxons and the Danes the tree was sacred, thought to contain a spirit or Goddess. To take a part of a tree would require gaining permission from the spirit or Goddess, lest she take revenge on the offending person.

Most of the Elder tree is poisonous, containing high levels of cyanide. Finds at York and Hedeby

Figs - Most written references to figs are biblical. Seeds found at Winchester in 11th century. It is possible they were imported, if not grown, along with other dried fruits as they were also found at York.

Grapes - Grown in Britain to some extent toward the end of the period, primarily to make wine. Probably only grown by the wealthy and monasteries. Finds at York, London, Hamwih (Southampton) and Hedeby - possibly imported.

Used as blessings at the coronation of Aethelred II, along with apples.

Hawthorn Berries - The name comes from the Old English 'haga' meaning hedge. It is the tree most mentioned in Saxon boundary charters. Finds at York and Hedeby

Hazel/cob nuts - Hazel comes from the Old English 'haesel', meaning 'hat'. Widespread finds of split and burnt nuts at York, Uppakra, Kaupang, Oseberg, Lejre and Hedeby.

Myrtle - Found at York and Hedeby. Used to spice beer and mead and mentioned in Leechdom as a light drink for lung disease.

Peaches - Archeological evidence at Hedbey only. Potential hint at on going trade? They are mentioned in Leechdoms, and in writings from further south in Switzerland and France. If used at all would be expensive and rare.

Pears - From the Old English word 'pere'. There is evidence from late in the period from Winchester and its mentioned in Leechdoms, however probably rare.

Pine Nuts - Referenced in leechdoms, but also imported to Britain by the Romans, so could still have been available to Anglo Saxons

Plums - Stones found in remains at York and Gloucestershire indicate that they were eaten whole. Also found at London, Hedeby and Birka.

Raspberries - Finds at York, Hedeby, Birka, Kaupang. Often listed as Hindberry

Rosehips - Possibly a famine food. Rose flowers were used in cooking and making oils.

Rowan - Widespread finds at Dublin, York, Uppakra, Kaupang, Lejre and hedeby

Wild Strawberries - From the Old English word "streawberige", meaning the berry associated with the straw, for unknown reason. Finds at York, Hedeby and Kaupang. Small and white, not like the large modern ones.

Sloes - From the Old English 'slah'. Stones at York, London and Gloucestershire. Also one of the most common fruit finds at Hedeby.

Walnuts - York, hedeby and Oseberg, possibly imported as nuts or oil from France.

Vegetables

Beetroot - Cultivated for its leaves and as animal feed. Found at York and Winchester and mentioned in Leechdoms.

Broad Beans - Finds at York, Hedeby and Lejre. Probably dried and turned into meal, as well as used to bulk out flour in times of famine.

Cabbage/kale (Loose Leaf) - Finds at York and seeds found at Hamwit

Carrots - Red, purple, black or white, but not orange. Orange wasn't cultivated till the 17th century. Seeds found at late Saxon sites in Winchester and Gloucestershire, as well as York.

Celery - Known in Britain since the Romans. Finds at York and Hedeby. The Winchester monk Ælfric Bata suggests it was cooked and eaten daily.

Cress (water) - Effective against scurvy. Finds at York, Ireland and Oseberg

Fennel - Finds at York and Winchester, but known since the Romans. One of the plants invoked in the pagan Anglo-Saxon 'Nine Herbs Charm'

Leeks - Finds at York. Written in runes on several items. Mentioned in Leechdoms as part of an eye salve with garlic, wine and cow bile, a combination now thought to kill MRSA.

Nettles - Taken from the Old English word 'noedl' meaning "needle." Mentioned in the nine herbs charm as protection against "elf-shot"; mysterious pains in humans or livestock caused by the arrows of the elven folk. Sap can be used as rennet to curdle milk into cheese and nettles eaten in soup or made into tea and beer. Finds at York, Uppakra, Kaupang, Birka and Oseberg.

Mushrooms - Little to no evidence, but seems likely due to the high nutritional content and the ease of drying for long term storage. References made to truffles.

Onions (white) - Spring onions and shallots - Mentioned as an answer in an Anglo Saxon riddle. A staple food, eaten daily in soups and salads. Hung in doorways to protect against infection.

Parsnips - Used to treat asthma. A staple food, eaten daily. Finds at York.

Peas - Dried and ground into meal and bread and added to porridge, pottage and stew. Finds at York, Birka, Kaupang and Lejre

Radish - Introduced to England by the Romans. Mentioned over 20 times in Leechcrafts as a treatment for many things, including depression, heartburn, wind and indigestion.

Rocket - Mentioned in Leechdoms.

Seaweed - Probable that this was eaten in coastal areas.

Spinach - Found at York.

Turnips - From the Old English 'neep'. Turnips, along with parsnips were important staples before potatoes came along. Finds at York and Uppakra

White goosefoot - Finds at York, Birka and Lejre. Seeds thought to be eaten in Dublin.

Grains

An important staple, whether used to thicken stews and pottages, eaten as porridge or fermented into beer, to make water safer to drink.

Barley - Used for porridge, breads and brewing. Finds at York, Hedeby, Uppakra, Birka, Kaupang, Lejre, Lofoten

Hops - Used in beer/ale brewing. Finds at York, Hedeby, Birka, Kaupang

Flax/linseed - Cultivated at Norfolk and York. Mainly for making linen and nets etc, but in Birka seeds have been found in bread. Seeds were also found in the intestinal tract of an Anglo Saxon skeleton.

Lentils - Finds from late in the period and mentioned in leechdoms as 'a sort of pea called lentils'

Oats - Widely grown as animal and human food. Ground into meal and used to make porridge, stew and pottage. Finds at York, Hedeby, Uppakra, Kaupang, Lejre

Rye - Commonly found at York, Portsmouth, Canterbury, Norfolk, Hedeby, Uppakra, Kaupang, Lejre. Though in Britain popularity dies down toward the end of the period for other grains that grew easier.

Spelt - Finds in Gloucestershire, Canterbury, Buckden down and Hamwit. Present in the East of England during Roman times, but disappears in the 5th century

Wheat - Processed into flour to make bread. Finds at York, Hedeby, Uppakra, Birka, Kaupang, Lejre

Dairy

Butter - Probably made from Cow's milk. More acidic and salty than modern butter to aid storage. Recipes found in Leechdoms. Churns found at Lund. Mostly used for cooking.

Cheese (Cottage, Goat, sheep, soft, hard white/yellow) - Could be made as a by-product to butter, using the leftover buttermilk. Can be salted or smoked to aid preservation. Hard cheese probably reserved for the wealthy, with fresh, soft, cheese being made by any household with their own animals.

Eggs (Chicken, Duck, Goose, Gull) - Recipes in Leechdoms for omelettes and custards. Finds at Barfriston and Holywell row.

Lard - Mentioned in sagas and leechdoms. Used in cooking.

Milk (Goat, Sheep) - Cow's milk was considered bad for human consumption. Mostly used to make cheese and soured milk.

Suet - Mentioned in leechdoms.

Whey - A by product of cheese making. Can be used in making pickles and bread.

Meat

Fresh meat, particularly large roasting joints, would have probably been reserved for special occasions or the wealthy. Dried meat and offal would be far more common, though probably far from a daily occurrence. Sausages date back to at least the Romans and there are a few references that may indicate there availability to the Vikings and Saxons

Badger - Mentioned in Leechdoms. Finds at Flaxengate, Portchester, Ramsbury, West Stow.

Beaver - From the Old English Beofor. Finds at Ramsbury and West Stow.

Beef - One of the most common archeological meat finds. Probably a high status food. At the time known as Cu, or modern cow. The word beef was not used until after the Normans.

Chicken - Much smaller than modern birds. Kept for eggs and meat since at least the iron age. Finds at Ramsbury, Flaxengate, and Exeter.

Deer - From the Old English 'Deor'. Lots of evidence of deer in the archeological record and mentioned in Aelfric's colloquy.

Duck - From the Old English 'Duce'. Finds at Hamwih West Stow, Ipswitch, Medmerry farm (Sussex), Exeter and a small amount at Flaxengate.

Goat - Famously mentioned in the Norse sagas. Not much archeological evidence, due to possible confusion with sheep bones.

Goose - Finds at Farthing down (Surrey), West Stow, Ipswitch, Medmerry farm (Sussex), Ramsbury and Exeter.

Hare - From the Old English Hara. Mentioned in Leechdoms, as well as Aelfric's colloquy. Finds at York and Portchester.

Horse - Probably only eaten by the poor and seen as uncivilised. Finds at Ramsbury, Andover, Sedgeford, Southampton, York and Hamwih.

Human - A less talked about source of food. Though obviously forbidden, during times of famine this was certainly a source of protein.

Lamb/Mutton - Mainly kept for milk and wool, sheep would have been eaten as a secondary source. Finds at Portchester, West Stow, Hamwih and King's Lynn and mentioned in legal documents and Leechdoms.

Peacock - Domesticated on large estates. Bones found on the Gokstad Viking ship and at Thetford.

Pork - Known as 'Swin' or modern swine. With no secondary uses a pig would have been used solely for its meat. A Saxon swineherd who looked after his lords pigs was entitled to one pig and it's entrails, presumably to use for making sausage casings.

Pigeon - Finds at Flaxengate, West Stow, Exeter, Portchester and Kings Lynn.

Swan - Finds at Flaxengate and West Stow.

Wild birds (gulls, buzzards, starlings, jackdaws, ravens etc) - Finds at Hamwih, Flaxengate and West Stow

Fish

Eaten by people of all status' in society, who had access to them. Bottom dwellers, like lobster and prawns were probably only eaten by the very poor. A large amount of these would have been preserved before being consumed, by drying, salting and smoking.

Bass - Finds at Hamwih, Exeter (late Saxon period) & Great Yarmouth

Bream - Find at Hamwih. Probably kept in man made fish ponds by the wealthy.

Cod - A common Find at many sites. Probably preserved/salted in Norway and exported. Finds at York, Hamwih, Exeter (late Saxon period), Flaxengate (late Saxon period), Durham, Northampton, King's lynn, and Great Yarmouth

Eel - Finds at York, Hamwih, Exeter (late Saxon period) & Great Yarmouth

Haddock - A common Find at York,Exeter (late Saxon period), Flaxengate (late Saxon period) & Great Yarmouth

Herring - Commonly found in Southern Scandinavia and York & Great Yarmouth

Mackerel - Finds at York, Hamwih & Great Yarmouth

Molluscs (cockles, crabs, Limpets, Lobster, Mussels, Oysters, Periwinkles, Prawns, Scallops, winkles) - Often found in large numbers. Finds at York, Hamwih, Bishopstone, Sarre, Portchester castle, Poole, Mawgan porth, Gosport & Thetford

Perch - Finds at West Stow, York, Hedeby, Birka and Uppraka. Probably kept by Saxons in man made fish ponds by the wealthy.

Pike - Finds at West Stow, York, Hedeby, Birka and Uppraka. Probably kept by Saxons in man made fish ponds by the wealthy.

Plaice - Hamwih, Exeter (late Saxon period), Flaxengate (late Saxon period), Kings Lynn & Great Yarmouth

Porpoise - Known as a 'mereswine' or 'sea pig'.

Ray - York, Great Yarmouth, Hamwih

Salmon - York, Hamwih, Exeter (late Saxon period), Flaxengate (late Saxon period)

Shark - Flaxengate (late Saxon period), Hamwih, Great Yarmouth

Trout - Flaxengate (late Saxon period)

Zander - Frequent find at Birka

Herbs & spices

Aniseed - Among the spices said to have been left by Bede to his brethren. The herb 'Sweet cicely' is said to taste like aniseed and was probably also used for its flavour.

Bay Leaves - Mentioned in leechdoms. Used in cooking and brewing. Said to have slightly narcotic effects.

Caraway - Finds at York and Denmark.

Comfrey - Mentioned in leechdoms. Used as a poultice for healing wounds and bruises. Now known to cause liver damage.

Chervil - Related to parsley. The name Chervil is Anglo-Norman.

Chicory - Finds at Hedeby. Related to the dandelion and bitter tasting. Roots used as a coffee substitute.

Cinnamon - Among the spices said to have been left by Bede to his brethren. Rare and expensive import.

Coriander - Finds at Fyrkat and York. Listed in Leechdoms.

Cumin - Found at Oseberg. Heavily referenced in the Leechdoms.

Dandelion - Adapted by the Saxons from the Norman 'dent de lion'. Used for it root, leaves and flowers.

Dill - Finds at York. From the Old English 'Dylle' meaning to lull, due to its soothing ability. Mentioned in Leechdoms as an anti witchcraft measure.

Elderflower - It was thought that if you burned elder wood you would see the Devil, but if you planted elder by your house it would keep the Devil away. Elder trees were the sources of many coloured dyes; Blue and purple from the berries; yellow and green from the leaves; grey and black from the bark.

Most of the Elder tree is poisonous, containing high levels of cyanide. Finds at York and Hedeby

Fennel - Finds at York, Winchester, Kaupang and Lofoten. Leechdoms suggest adding to wine and other mentions made to adding to bread.

Garlic (wild) - from Old English '*garleac*' meaning "spear-leek". Has powerful antibacterial properties.

Garlic mustard (jack-by-the-hedge,

Ginger - Referenced in Leechdoms and left by Bede to his brethren. Imported, so probably rare and expensive.

Gorse - From the Old English 'Gorst' meaning waste. Smells like coconut. Can be used to make wine or dried and used as fire lighting tinder.

Horse radish - Finds on the Oseberg ship and mentioned in Leechdoms.

Juniper - Finds at Kaupang and Lofoten, used in beer and cooking

Marjoram - Related to Oregano. Reasonably cold hardy. Mentioned by a tenth century Irish hermit.

Meadowsweet - From the Old English word Meduwyrt, indicating its connection with brewing mead. Finds at York and Kaupang.

Mint - Mentioned in Leechdoms as part of a recipe for a sauce and a broth.

Mustard - Finds at York (black mustard), Oseberg and Denmark (yellow mustard)

Parsley - Eaten daily according to Aelfric's Colloquy.

Peppercorns - A highly regarded, imported spice. Mentioned in lots of leechdoms and used with salt, much as we do today.

Rosemary - Used in Shamanic rituals and to enhance the effects of beer. High dosage may have been used to cause the frenzied rage of a berserker.

Rose hips - From the Old English 'Hiop'. Scandinavian folklore suggests that the Vikings fueled themselves on Rose Hips before going on raids.

Sage - Mentioned in leechdoms, including a recipe for a sage omelette and as an infusion for fevers and oral infections.

Salt - Mainly used in preservation of meat, fish, cheese and butter.

Soapwort - Mainly known for its use as a gentle soap. Mix roots and leaves with hot water, to produce a lather. Although an overdose can cause nausea, diarrhoea & vomiting, it does have uses in beer brewing, to produce a good head and in some foodstuffs.

Sorrel - Finds at Kaupang, Lofoten and Lejre. Mentioned in leechdoms

Sweet gale (bog Myrtle) - Finds in York and Hedeby. Used as a flavouring in Beer and mead. Leechdoms suggest using to treat headaches.

Tarragon - Mentioned in Leechdoms. As the modern culinary herb is 'French Tarragon' it's possible it was less commonly used in Saxon England. Can be used to treat toothache.

Thyme - Originally spread throughout Europe by the Romans. Mentioned in leechdoms, so may have been used for food, as well as for its medicinal benefits.

Yarrow - From the Old English 'gearwe'. Used in brewing beer for its flavour and its preserving qualities, before hops were common. In many places it was used to Staunch bleeding. Finds at York, Lofoten and Kaupang.

Drinks

Beer (ealu) - A weak beer would have been drunk daily by many, due to being safer to drink than water. The sap from the sycamore tree was sometimes used to sweeten and strengthen a brew.

The flavour and strength varied depending on the skill and preference of each brewer. Before hops became widely available, foraged herbs such as yarrow, bog myrtle and rosemary were used to flavour and preserve.

Cider - If known to the Saxons it may have been what is referenced as 'beor'.

Herbal Teas - 'wort drinks' or tisanes are mentioned in Leechdoms and other sources, without any method or recipe. Presumably boiling water was deemed safer to drink.

Mead (meodu) - Perhaps the most commonly thought of drink from the early medieval period. References are everywhere from the famously named 'meadhalls' to writings such as Beowulf and the Norse sagas.

With honey being such an expensive commodity it is probable that drinking mead was kept for special occasions and ceremony.

Wine - Wine made from grapes was not common to the Saxons and thus was very expensive. It was mainly produced for personal consumption by the lord and his retinue and later for the monks in the monasteries.

Other

Honey - An expensive commodity, saved for only the wealthy or those stupid enough to raid wild bee hives. Those that kept bee's did so in 'Skeps', an Old English word, meaning basket. Generally the bees were killed in order to obtain the honey within. Bee Churls belonged to the lowest rank of freemen and had to pay rent on taxable bees, which may have been paid in the form of honey.

Oil (Flax/Linseed, Olive, Rapeseed, walnut) - Mentioned in Leechdoms. Imported and used in cooking

Vinegar (cider, malt) - Mainly used in curdling milk to make cheese and pickling veg and fish. There are also references to marinading beef in vinegar and herbs.

Further reading list

I highly recommend the following books and sources for further research.

Food & Drink inn Anglo-Saxon England - Debbie Banham

The Meadhall - Stephen Pollington

Making mead - Brian Acton & Peter Duncan

Leechcraft - Stephen Pollington

The Medieval cookbook - Maggie Black

An early meal - Daniel Serra & Hanna Tunberg

A Heathen guide to cooking, baking & brewing - Craig & Emma Brooks

Another Heathen guide to cooking, baking & brewing - Craig & Emma Brooks

Anglo Saxon food & drink - Ann Hagen

The world history of beekeeping and honey hunting - Ethel Eva Crane

River cottage handbook no.13 - curing & smoking by Steven Lamb

Aspects of Anglo-Saxon magic - Bill Griffiths

Vickery's folk flora - Roy Vickery

About the Author

Craig lives in Swindon, Wiltshire with his wife Emma and daughter Ocean. When he isn't working Craig likes to cook and grow his own food. He is a member of the group Ulfrahfnar in the Vikings society, portraying an Anglo Saxon peace hostage named Aethelwulf.

Printed in Great Britain
by Amazon